walk the l

ORIGINAL MOTION PICTURE SON(

GW00372704

Published by
Wise Publications
14/15 Berners Street, London, W1T 3LJ, England.

Exclusive distributors:
Music Sales Limited
Distribution Centre, Newmarket Road,
Bury St Edmunds, Suffolk, IP33 3YB, England.

Music Sales Pty Limited
20 Resolution Drive, Caringbah, NSW 2229, Australia.

Order No. AM985490   ISBN 1-84609-525-5

This book © Copyright 2006 Wise Publications,
a division of Music Sales Limited.

Unauthorised reproduction of any part of this publication by
any means including photocopying is an infringement of copyright.

Music arranged by Andy Keenan.
Music processed by Paul Ewers Music Design.
Edited by Chris Harvey.
Printed in the EU.

www.musicsales.com

This publication is not authorised for sale in
the United States of America and / or Canada

Wise Publications
part of The Music Sales Group
London / New York / Paris / Sydney / Copenhagen / Berlin / Madrid / Tokyo

Get Rhythm

Words & Music by Johnny Cash

rhy - thm,   when you   get the blues.___   1. A lit - tle
                                                                                                     2. Well I

shoe shine boy___ he nev - er gets low down___ but he's got the dir - ti - est
sat and I___ lis - tened to the shoe shine boy___ and I thought___ I was gonna

job in town,___   bend - ing low___ at the peo - ples feet___ on a
jump for joy,___   slapped on the shoe po - lish left and right,___ he took the

wind - y cor - ner of a dir - ty street.___ When I asked___ him while he
shoe shine rag_____ and he held it tight.___ He stopped once___ to wipe the

To Coda

a jump - ing rhy - thm makes you feel so fine___ it - 'll
it only cost a dime___ just a nickle a shoe___ it does a

shake all your trou - ble from your wor - ried mind,___ get rhy - thm
mil - lion dol - lars worth of good for you,___ get rhy - thm

when you get the blues.___
when you get the blues.___

I Walk The Line

Words & Music by Johnny Cash

ends out for the tie that binds, be - cause you're

mine, I walk the line.

Mmm.

2. I find it
4. You've got a

Wildwood Flower

Traditional
Arranged by A.P. Carter

red and the lil - lies___ so fair.
heart, in each crown I___ will sway.

And the myr - tle___ so bright with the
When I woke from___ my dream - ing my

em - 'rald dew,___ the pale and the
id - ols were clay,___ all por - tion of

1.

lead - er___ and eyes look light blue.   2. I will dance,
love___ had

Verse 3:
Oh, he taught me to love him and promised to love
And to cherish me over all others above
How my heart is now wand'ring no mis'ry can't tell
He's left me no warning, no words of farewell.

Verse 4:
Oh, he taught me to love him and called me his flower
That was blooming to cheer him though life's dreary hour
How I long to see him and regret the dark hour
He's gone and this pale wildwood flower.

Lewis Boogie

Music by Jerry Lee Lewis

My name is Jer-ry Lee Le-wis, I'm from Lou-si-a-na. Gon-na do a lit-tle boo-gie on this here_ pia-no. Do-ing migh-ty fine,_ gon-na

make you shake; gon - na make you do it, make you do it, 'till it breaks. It's called the

Le - wis boo - gie, in the Le - wis way. Lord, I

do my lit - tle boo - gie woo - gie ev - 'ry day.

Ring Of Fire

Words & Music by Merle Kilgore & June Carter

Love_____ is a burn-ing thing,
Taste_____ of love is sweet,

and it makes_____ a fi - ry ring.
when hearts_____ like ours___ beat.

Bound_____ by wild de - sires,
I fell for you like a child,

I fell in___ to a ring of
oh_____ but the fire went

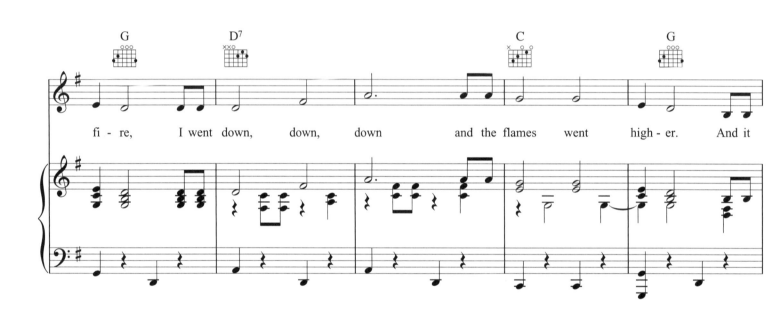

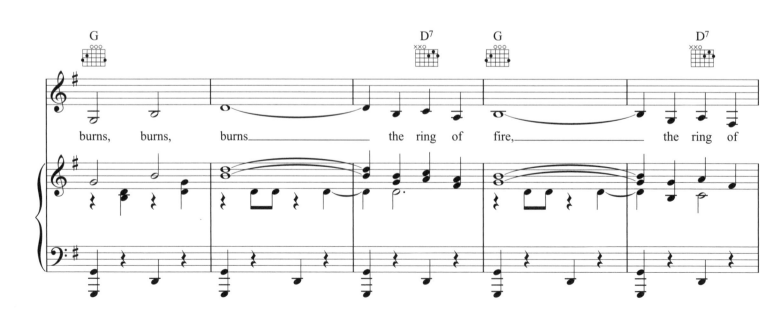

26

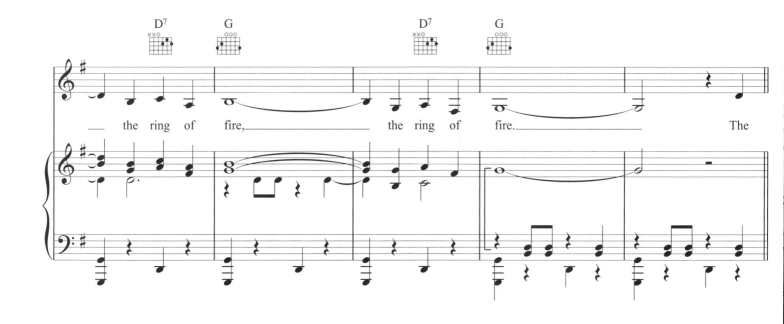

the ring of fire, _____ the ring of fire. _____ The

Coda

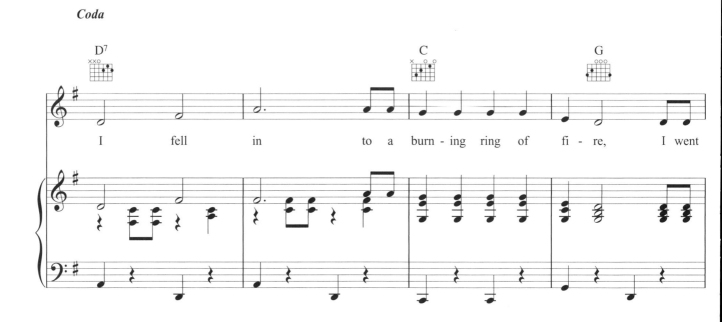

I fell in to a burn - ing ring of fi - re, I went

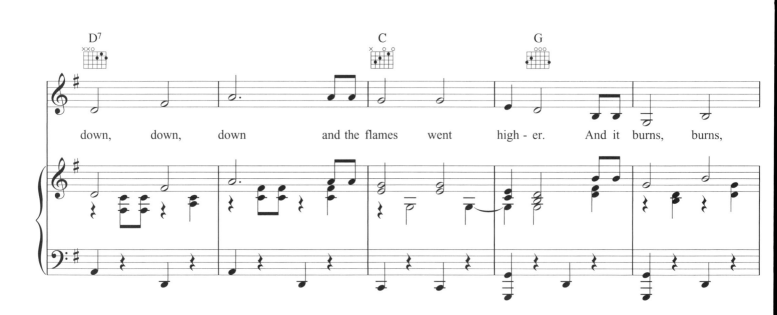

down, down, down and the flames went high - er. And it burns, burns,

28

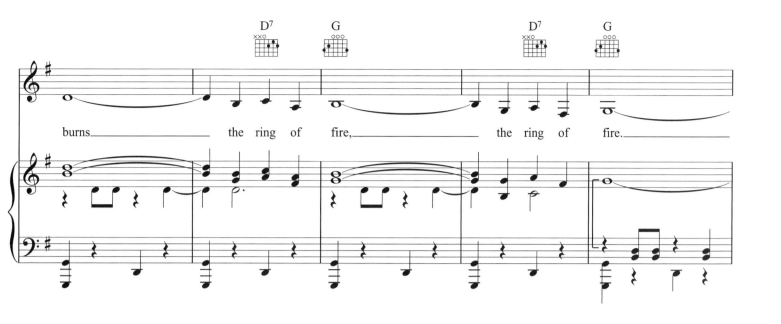

burns the ring of fire, the ring of fire.

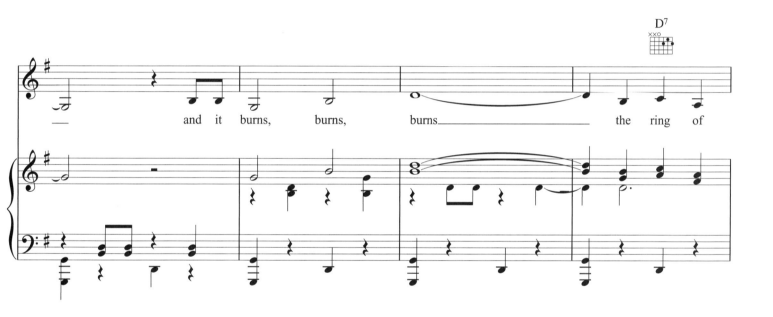

and it burns, burns, burns the ring of

Repeat and fade

fire, the ring of fire. The ring of

You're My Baby

Words & Music by Johnny Cash

need it to run my fin-gers through, 'cause you're my ba - by,___ you're my
they don't catch me I'll spend it on you, 'cause you're my ba - by, you're my

su - gar, don't_ mean may - be,___ you're my
su - gar, don't_ mean may - be,___ you're my

ba - by.___
ba - by.___

1, 3. **2, 4.**

2, 4.Well,

(Verses 3-4 see block lyric)

Oh, ba - by,

ba - by,___ you're___ my ba - by.___ Well, I don't mean

Verse 3:

Well, I got a guitar, got six strings
And a picker to make them ring
Every string's gotta know what to do
'Cause I'm gonna serenade you
'Cause you're my baby, you're my sugar,
Don't mean maybe, you're my baby.

Verse 4:

Well, I had a girl who said she's mine
But she run around on me all the time
Now she's gone and I'm glad we're through
'Cause I-I'm plum-flipped over you
'Cause you're my baby, you're my sugar
Don't mean maybe, you're my baby.

Cry! Cry! Cry!

Words & Music by Johnny Cash

time when I would try, try, try, 'Cause

when the lights have lost their glow you'll cry, cry,

cry. Soon your sug - ar dad - dies will

all be gone. You'll wake up some

Folsom Prison Blues

Words & Music by Johnny Cash

Verse 4:

I bet there's rich folks eatin' in a fancy dining car.

They're prob'ly drinkin' coffee and smokin' big cigars,

But I know I had it comin', I know I can't be free,

But those people keep a-movin', and that's what tortures me.

Verse 5: Instrumental

Verse 6:

Well, if they freed me from prison, if that railroad train was mine,

I bet I'd move it on a little further down the line,

Far from Folsom Prison, that's where I want to stay,

And I'd let that lonesome whistle blow my blues away.

That's All Right

Words & Music by Arthur Crudup

♩ = 100

Moderately bright

1. Well,

that's all right,___ Ma - ma, that's all right for you.
(2). Ma - ma she done told me, Pa - pa done told me too,
(Verse 3 instrumental)
(Verses 4 & 5 see block lyric)

That's all right,___ Ma - ma, just___ a - ny way you do.
Son that gal you're fool - in' with she ain't no good for you, but } That's all

Verse 4:

I'm leavin' town tomorrow, leavin' town for sure.
Then you won't be bothered with me hangin' 'round your door.
But that's all right, that's all right.
That's all right Mama, any way you do.

Verse 5:

Vocal ad. lib.
But that's all right, that's all right.
That's all right Mama, any way you do.

Juke Box Blues

Words & Music by Helen Carter & Maybelle Carter

Original key F#

walked in - to a honk - ey tonk - ey just the oth - er day, I

43

44

Well, the man on the fid-dle he must have got tired, I

did-n't hear him say, 'cause he cut loose on the steel gui-tar___ and the

juke box ran a - way.

It Ain't Me Babe

Words & Music by Bob Dylan

lightly on the ground. I'm

not the one you want, babe, I will only let you

down. You say you're lookin'

for some-one who'll pro-mise nev-er to part, some-

51

Verse 3:
Go melt back into the night, babe
Everything inside is made of stone
There's nothing in here moving
An' anyway I'm not alone.

You say you're looking for someone
Who'll pick you up each time you fall
To gather flowers constantly
An' to come each time you call
A lover for your life an' nothing more.

But it ain't me *etc*.

Home Of The Blues

Words & Music by Johnny Cash, Glen Douglas & Lillie McAlpin

Just a-round the cor-ner there's heart-ache, down the street that lo-sers use. If you can wade in through the tear-

wel - come at the home of the blues.___

D.S. al Coda

Coda

Yeah, you're gon-na find me at the home of the blues.

Milk Cow Blues

Words & Music by Kokomo Arnold

need you're dad - dy's lov ing help some - day.   Well,

then you're gon - na be sor - ry   for treat-ing me   this   way.

Well,_____ be - lieve me, don't that sun look good go - ing down? Well, be-

-lieve me, don't that sun look good go - ing down?

count the days_ I'm gone. I'm gon-na leave,_____ you're gon-na

need you're lov-ing dad-dy's help some-day. Well,

then you're gon-na be sor-ry for treat-ing me this

way.

I'm A Long Way From Home

Words & Music by Hank Cochran

Cocaine Blues

Words & Music by T. J. "Red" Arnall

Verse 2:
Got up next mornin' and I grabbed that gun
Took a shot of cocaine and away I run
Made a good run but I ran too slow
They overtook me down in Juarez, Mexico.

Verse 3:
Late in the hot joints takin' the pills
In walked the sheriff from Jericho Hill
He said, "Willy Lee, your name is not Jack Brown
You're the dirty hack that shot your woman down."

Verse 4:
Said, "Yes, oh yes, my name is Willy Lee
If you've got the warrant just a-read it to me
Shot her down because she made me sore
I thought I was her daddy but she had five more."

Verse 5:
When I was arrested I was dressed in black
They put me on a train and they took me back
Had no friend for to go my bail
They slapped my dried up carcass in that county jail.

Verse 6:
Early next mornin', 'bout a half past nine
I spied the sheriff coming down the line
Ah, and he coughed as he cleared his throat
He said come on you dirty hack into that district court.

Verse 7:
Into the courtroom my trial began
Where I was handled by twelve honest men
Just before the jury started out
I saw that little judge commence to look about.

Verse 8:
In about five minutes in walked the man
Holding the verdict in his right hand
The verdict read murder in the first degree
I hollered, "Lawdy Lawdy, have a mercy on me."

Verse 9:
The judge he smiled as he picked up his pen
Ninety-nine years in the Folsom pen
Ninety-nine years underneath that ground
I can't forget the day I shot that bad bitch down.

Jackson

Words & Music by Billy Edd Wheeler & Gaby Rogers

Moderately

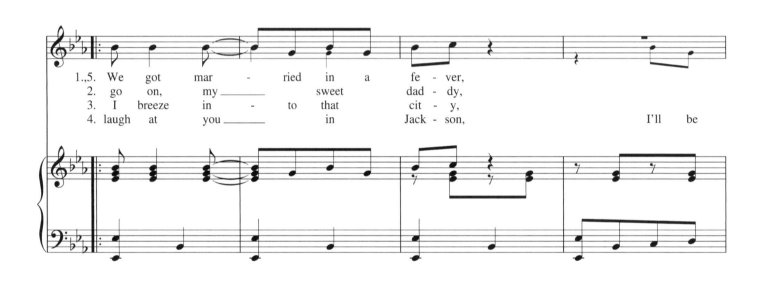

1.,5. We got mar - ried in a fe - ver,
2. go on, my ___ sweet dad - dy,
3. I breeze in - to that cit - y,
4. laugh at you ___ in Jack - son, I'll be

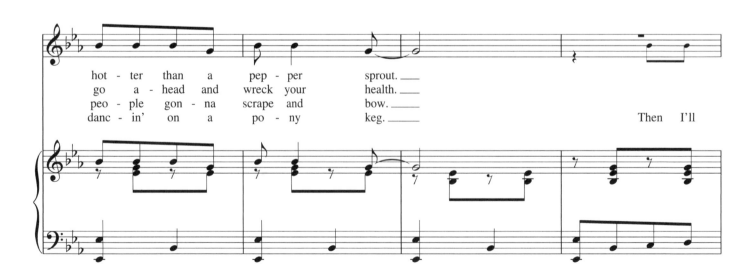

hot - ter than a pep - per sprout. ___
go a - head and wreck your health. ___
peo - ple gon - na scrape and bow. ___
danc - in' on a po - ny keg. ___ Then I'll

We been talk - in' 'bout Jack - son
Play your hand _____ like a lov - er man, _____ make a
All them wom - en gon - na beg me, _____
lead you 'round town _____ like a scold - ed hound _____ with your

Ab/Bb   Eb

ev - er since the fire went out. (He:) I'm goin' to
big fool of your - self. Go on to
teach 'em what they don't know how. I'm goin' to
tail tucked be - tween your legs. So, go on down to

Ab

Jack - son, _____ gon - na mess a - round. _____
Jack - son, _____ comb your hair. _____
Jack - son, _____ turn loose my coat. _____
Jack - son, _____ you big talk - in' man. _____

Yeah,   I'm goin'   to
He: Got - ta   snow - ball
I'm   goin'   to
I'll   be   wait - in'   in

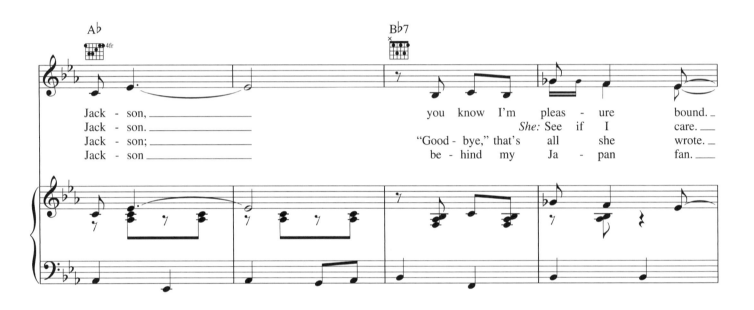

Jack - son,   you know I'm pleas - ure   bound.
Jack - son.   *She:* See if I   care. __
Jack - son;   "Good - bye," that's all she   wrote.
Jack - son   be - hind my Ja - pan   fan. __

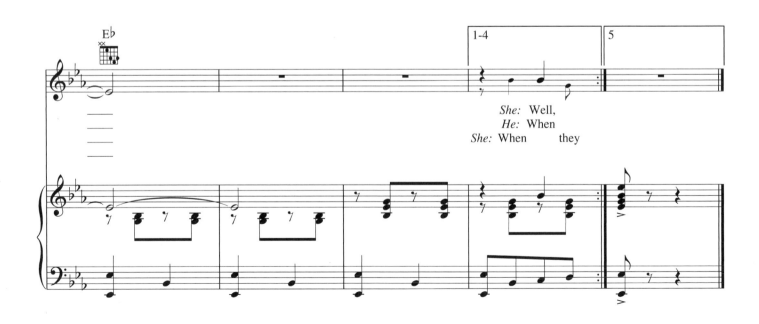

She: Well,
He: When
She: When they

23456789
9/08(166809)